sanskrita varṇamālā Garland of syllables Book three: guṇitākṣaram & samyuktākṣaram

Abhidheya Devī Dāsī
Bhakti Kids Saṅgha

Varnamāla- garland of syllables book three
ISBN: 978-1-326-44546-1

alice.goulding@googlemail.com
www.youtube.com/c/Bhaktikidssangha
www.facebook.com/Bhaktikidssangha
Instagram: @bhakti_kids_sangha

Acknowledgements:
A.C. Bhaktivedanta Swami Prabhupāda
Kadamba Kanana Swami
Kedhār Eswaran - Sanskrita Bharati
Lajjāvatī Devī dāsī - The Hare Krishna School
Prāna Das & Candrakoti mataji
My wonderful students

Sanskrita Varṇamālā Introduction

In book one we learned vowels स्वरः svaraḥ and in book two we learned consonants व्यञ्जनम् vyañjanam.
Please refer to them for detailed explanations on these sounds and their groups and features.

In book three we will build on our knowledge of the varṇamālā and move towards more fluent reading and writing, broadening our understanding of how sounds or phonemes come together and are expressed.

In book three we will look in detail at dependant vowels and compound consonants.
Transliteration and English translations are provided to allow you to read this book no matter where you are in your learning journey.

vowels स्वराः svarāḥ

अ  अम्बा	आ  आम्रम्	इ  इन्द्रधनुः	ई  ईश्वरः
उ  उलूकः	ऊ  ऊर्णा	ऋ  ऋषिः	ॠ
ऌ	ॡ	ए  एडः	ऐ  ऐश्वर्यम्
ओ 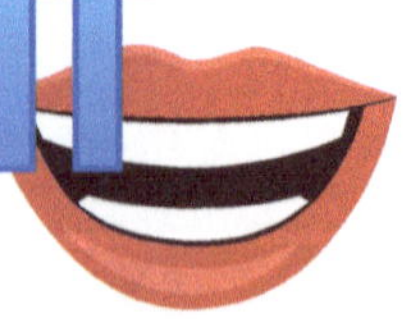 ओष्ठः	औ  औषधम्	Vowels are independant sounds that can be pronounced on their own	Transliteration of all these sounds, words and information on groupings are in book 1 & 2
अं	 मन्दिरं	अः	 कृष्णः

Consonants व्यञ्जनानि vyañjanāni

क कमलम्	ख खगः	ग गुरुः	घ घटी	ङ अङ्गः
च चन्द्रः	छ छत्रम्	ज जपः	झ झिल्ली	ञ मञ्जरी
ट नटः	ठ पृष्ठम्	ड दण्डः	ढ ढक्का	ण कृष्णः
त तिलकम्	थ कथा	द दीपः	ध धनुः	न नक्षत्रम्
प पुष्पम्	फ फलम्	ब बालः	भ भोजनम्	म माता
य योगः	र राधा	ल लता	व वस्त्रम्	Consonants are pronounced with vowels
श शास्त्रम्	ष पुरुषः	स सूर्यः	ह हरिणः	Transliteration of all sounds, words and information on groups are in book 1 & 2

Phonemes in sanskrit

Phonemes are NOT letters, rather they are the smallest units of sound in a language that can distinguish meaning between words. In sanskrit, phonemes are very important as sanskrit is purely phonetic - meaning pronunciation matches what is written. In book one and two we learned all the vowel and consonant phonemes. In book three we will complete our elementary understanding of phonemes by learning dependant vowels and compound consonants.

In this English example we see the sound 'at' being added with a new phoneme in front of it, which changes the meaning and creates a new word altogether.

In this example we see the words are almost identical except for a change in vowel length changing the meaning from something related to the divine to vomit!

we see the words are almost identical again, a change in aspiration alters the meaning here! from non aspirated प् p to aspirated फ् ph this change in phoneme alters the meaning.

Dependant vowels & half syllables

गुणिताक्षरम् अर्धाक्षरम् च

guṇitākṣaram ardhākṣaram ca

क	क्	क्‍
क ka **Full syllable** **pūrṇākṣaram** **consonant** **contains a** **a vowel.**	क् k **Base Syllable** **mūlākṣaram** **For forming** **dependant vowels** **guṇitākṣaram**	क् k **Half Syllable** **ardhākṣaram** **forming compound** **consonants** **samyuktākṣaram**

A consonant or full syllable must contain a vowel to be complete as we saw in book two.
A base syllable is when a halanta (see the 'stopper' underneath क्) is added to a consonant, it removes the vowel providing a base to add any vowel from अ a to अः aḥ to create a new sound to form dependant vowels.
A half syllable is a broken or incomplete form of a consonant that does not contain a vowel they are used to form compound consonants.
We will study these concepts in detail in book three.

Dependant vowels
गुणिताक्षरम्
guṇitākṣaram

In Sanskrit, vowels and consonant phonemes want to work together to make new sounds and words.

Full-Form Vowels:

Vowels are independent sounds and can be pronounced on their own.

They are strong and independent. When they come at the beginning or end of a word, they stand in their full independant form, For example the first sound in the word anānasaḥ is short अ a so it is expressed in its full form अ a as we learned it in book one.

आ ā

आम्रम्

āmram

Mango

ऋ ṛ

ऋषिः

ṛṣiḥ

Sage

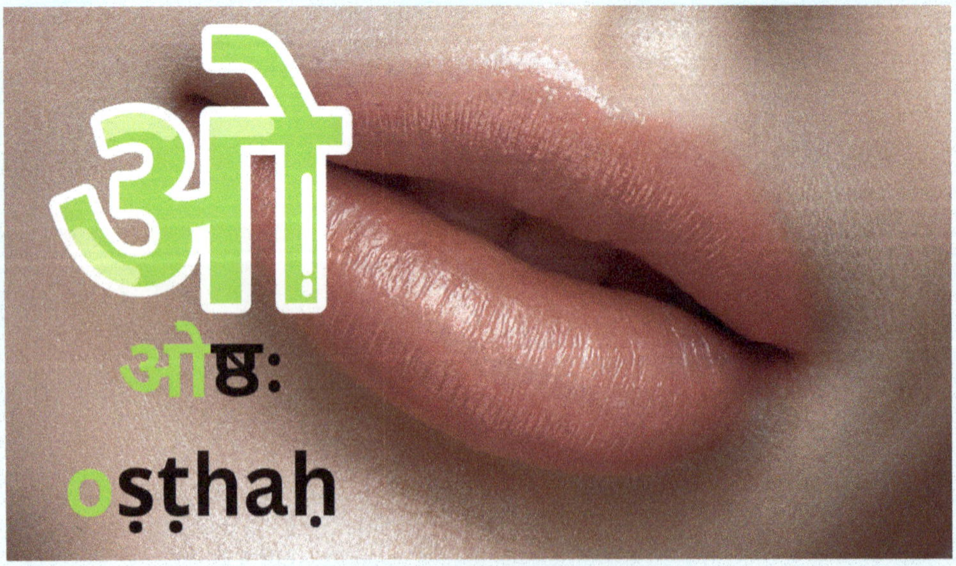

ओ o

ओष्ठः

oṣṭhaḥ

Lip

Here we see vowels at the beginning of words in their full independant form.

We see vowels in their full form only at the beginning or end of words, and we know that consonants must contain a vowel - so dependant vowels or gunitākṣaram गुणिताक्षरम् is when a consonant is paired with any of the vowels अ a to अः aḥ INSIDE a word.

in the middle of the above picture we see क् k has paired with long आ ā to create a new sound का kā in the word कालः kālaḥ (time) this is an example of dependant vowels.

Let us take two consonants that you are familiar with क् k and ग् g and see how they pair with all the vowels अ a to अः aḥ to create new sounds following a set pattern.

क् k
halanta - no vowel
क ka
full consonant

क ka
कमलम्
kamalam
Lotus

का kā
कालः
kālaḥ
Time

कि ki

किरणः

kiraṇaḥ

Dawn

की kī

कीटः

kīṭaḥ

Dawn

कु ku

कुण्डम्

kuṇḍam

Water Hole

कू kū
कूपी
kūpī
Bottle

कृ kṛ
कृष्णः
kṛṣṇaḥ
Krishna

कॢ kḷ
कॢप्तिः
kḷipaḥ
Success

क् + ए = के

केशा:

क्+ए+शा+आ+अ:

के ke

केशा:

keśāḥ

Hair

कै kai

कैरवम्

kairavam

White lotus

क् + ऐ = कै

कैरवम्

क्+ऐ+र्+अ+व्+अ+म्

क् + ओ = को

कोकिल:

क्+ओ+क्+इ+ल्+अ:

को ko

कोकिल:

kokilaḥ

Bird

कौ kau

कौस्तुभः

kaustu-
bhaḥ

Gem

कं kam

कंसः

kaṁsaḥ

Krishnas
Uncle

कः kaḥ

शुकः

śukaḥ

Parrot

क गुणिताक्षरम्

क्+अ= क
k + a = ka

क्+आ= का
k+ ā = kā

क्+इ= कि
k + i = ki

क्+ई= की
k + ī= kī

क्+उ= कु
k + u = ku

क्+ऊ= कू
k + ū = kū

क्+ऋ= कृ
k + ṛ = kṛ

क्+ॠ= कॄ
k + ṛ = kṛ

क्+ऌ= कॢ
k + ḷṛ = kḷṛ

क्+ए= के
k + e = ke

क्+ऐ= कै
k + ai = kai

क्+ओ= को
k + o = ko

क्+औ= कौ
k + au = kau

क्+अं= कं
k + aṁ = kaṁ

क्+अः= कः
k + aḥ = kaḥ

The base syllable in this case क् has a halanta this acts as a 'stopper' that drops the vowel we only see this at the end of words in sanskrit or like the table when we are adding new vowels to a consonant. Try reading through the sounds in order.

We have seen examples of the consonant क् paired with all the vowels with word examples and full split statergy of the individual sounds.

All base syllable forms of consonants क् k to ह् h can be paired with any vowel अ a to अः aḥ to create a new sound following these formulas (summarised in the above table).

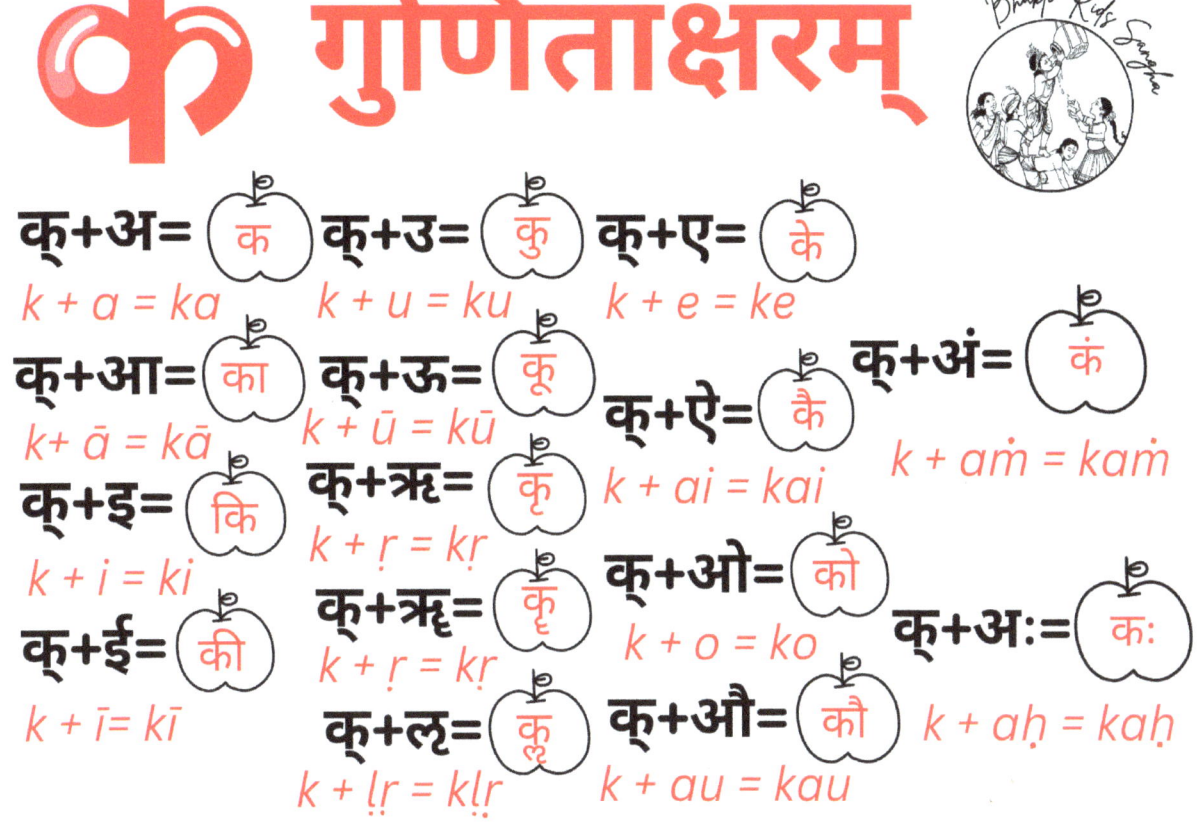

ग् g
halanta -
no vowel
ग ga
full
consonant

ग ga
गजः
gajaḥ
Elephant

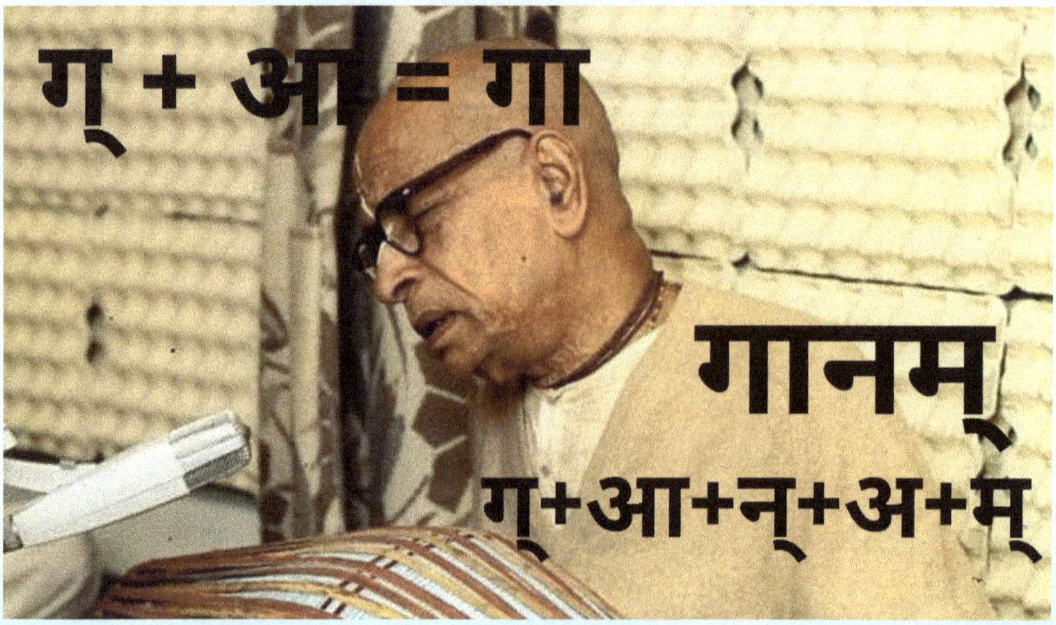

गा gā
गानम्
gānam
Song

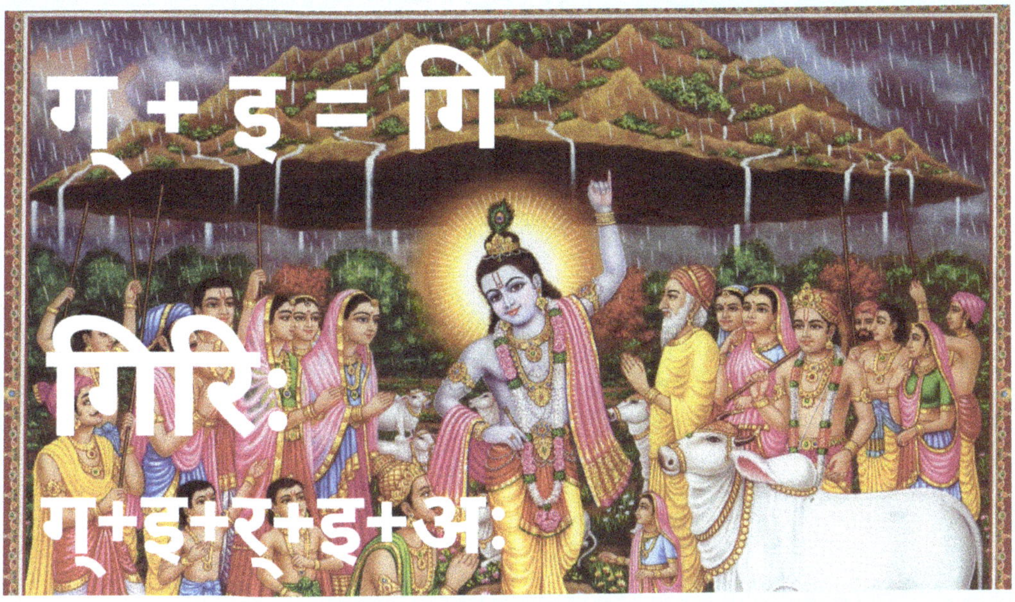

गि gi

गिरिः

girih̩

Hill

गी gī

गीतम्

gītam

Song

गु gu

गुरुः

guruḥ

Teacher

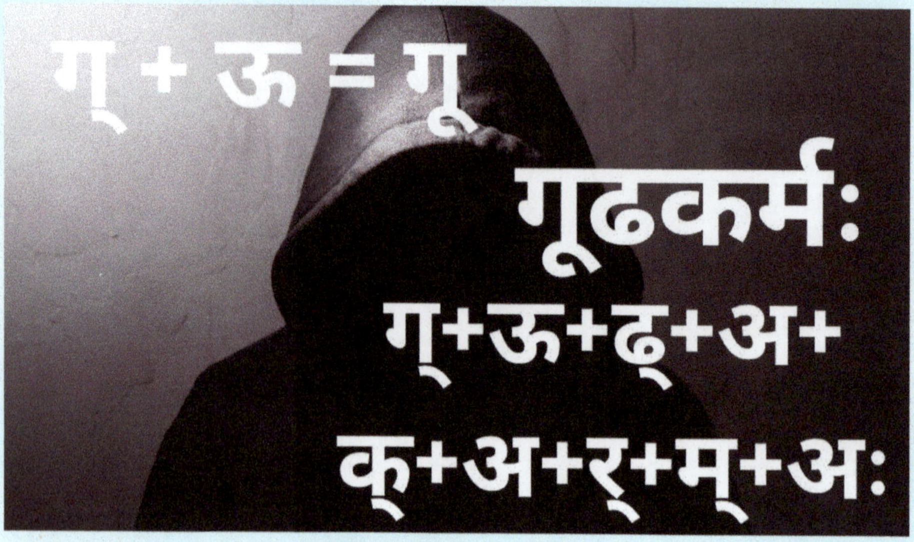

गू gū
गूढकर्मः
gūḍha-
karmaḥ
Secret
deed

गृ gṛ
गृहम्
gṛham
House

गे ge
गेहम्
geham
Home

गै gai
गैरिकम्
gairikam
Red Chalk

गो go
गोपी
gopī
Milk-maid

गौ gau
गौः
gauḥ
Cow

गं gam

खगं

khagaṁ

Bird

गः gaḥ

खगः

khagaḥ

Bird

ग गुणिताक्षरम्

ग्+अ= ग

ग्+आ= गा

ग्+इ= गि

ग्+ई= गी

ग्+उ= गु

ग्+ऊ= गू

ग्+ऋ= गृ

ग्+ॠ= गॄ

ग्+ऌ= गॢ

ग्+ए= गे

ग्+ऐ= गै

ग्+ओ= गो

ग्+औ= गौ

ग्+अं= गं

ग्+अः= गः

ग्

paired

with

all

vowels

अ - अः

ग गुणिताक्षरम्

ग्+अ= ग
g + a = ga

ग्+आ= गा
g + ā = gā

ग्+इ= गि
g + i = gi

ग्+ई= गी
g + ī= gī

ग्+उ= गु
g + u = gu

ग्+ऊ= गू
g + ū = gū

ग्+ऋ= गृ
g + ṛ = kṛ

ग्+ॠ= गॄ
g + ṝ = kṝ

ग्+ऌ= गॢ
g + ḷr = kḷr

ग्+ए= गे
g + e = ge

ग्+ऐ= गै
g + ai = gai

ग्+ओ= गो
g + o = go

ग्+औ= गौ
g + au = gau

ग्+अं= गं
g + aṁ = gaṁ

ग्+अः= गः
g + aḥ = gaḥ

we have seen detailed examples of the base consonant ग् g being combined with all the vowels अ a to अः aḥ to create a new sound. Try reading the sound combinations through and reading the example words. Try to memorise the sounds without transliteration and practise the written expressions on the sheets provided in this book. Photocopy the worksheets and practise regularly.

Now we will look at half syllables and compound consonants.

भ गुणिताक्षरम्

भ्+अ= भ

भ्+आ= भा

भ्+इ= भि

भ्+ई= भी

भ्+उ= भु

भ्+ऊ= भू

भ्+ऋ= भृ

भ्+ॠ= भॄ

भ्+ऌ= भॢ

भ्+ए= भे

भ्+ऐ= भै

भ्+ओ= भो

भ्+औ= भौ

भ्+अं= भं

भ्+अः= भः

Bhakti Kids Sangha

भ गुणिताक्षरम्

भ्+अ=

भ्+आ=

भ्+इ=

भ्+ई=

भ्+उ=

भ्+ऊ=

भ्+ऋ=

भ्+ॠ=

भ्+ऌ=

भ्+ए=

भ्+ऐ=

भ्+ओ=

भ्+औ=

भ्+अं=

भ्+अः=

Bhakti Kids Sangha

क गुणिताक्षरम्

क्+अ=

क्+आ=

क्+इ=

क्+ई=

क्+उ=

क्+ऊ=

क्+ऋ=

क्+ॠ=

क्+ऌ=

क्+ए=

क्+ऐ=

क्+ओ=

क्+औ=

क्+अं=

क्+अः=

Bhakti Kids Sangha

छ गुणिताक्षरम्

छ्+अ=

छ्+आ=

छ्+इ=

छ्+ई=

छ्+उ=

छ्+ऊ=

छ्+ऋ=

छ्+ॠ=

छ्+ऌ=

छ्+ए=

छ्+ऐ=

छ्+ओ=

छ्+औ=

छ्+अं=

छ्+अः=

Bhakti Kids Sangha

म गुणिताक्षरम्

म्+अ=

म्+आ=

म्+इ=

म्+ई=

म्+उ=

म्+ऊ=

म्+ऋ=

म्+ॠ=

म्+ऌ=

म्+ए=

म्+ऐ=

म्+ओ=

म्+औ=

म्+अं=

म्+अः=

त गुणिताक्षरम्

त्+अ=

त्+आ=

त्+इ=

त्+ई=

त्+उ=

त्+ऊ=

त्+ऋ=

त्+ॠ=

त्+ऌ=

त्+ए=

त्+ऐ=

त्+ओ=

त्+औ=

त्+अं=

त्+अः=

Bhakti Kids Sangha

ट गुणिताक्षरम्

ट्+अ=

ट्+आ=

ट्+इ=

ट्+ई=

ट्+उ=

ट्+ऊ=

ट्+ऋ=

ट्+ॠ=

ट्+ऌ=

ट्+ए=

ट्+ऐ=

ट्+ओ=

ट्+औ=

ट्+अं=

ट्+अः=

Bhakti Kids Sangha

ह गुणिताक्षरम्

ह्+अ=

ह्+आ=

ह्+इ=

ह्+ई=

ह्+उ=

ह्+ऊ=

ह्+ऋ=

ह्+ॠ=

ह्+ऌ=

क्+ए=

ह्+ऐ=

ह्+ओ=

ह्+औ=

ह्+अं=

ह्+अः=

Bhakti Kids Sangha

फ् गुणिताक्षरम्

फ्+अ=

फ्+आ=

फ्+इ=

फ्+ई=

फ्+उ=

फ्+ऊ=

फ्+ऋ=

फ्+ॠ=

फ्+ऌ=

फ्+ए=

फ्+ऐ=

फ्+ओ=

फ्+औ=

फ्+अं=

फ्+अः=

फ् गुणिताक्षरम्

Pha

फ्+अ= फ pha

फ्+आ= फा phā

फ्+इ= फि phi

फ्+ई= फी phī

फ्+उ= फु phu

फ्+ऊ= फू phū

फ्+ऋ= फृ phṛ

फ्+ॠ= फॄ phṝ

फ्+ऌ= फॢ phḷ

फ्+ए= फे phe

फ्+ऐ= फै phai

फ्+ओ= फो pho

फ्+औ= फौ phau

फ्+अं= फं phaṁ

फ्+अः= फः phaḥ

In summary:

Any base consonant can be paired with any vowel to create a new sound or phoneme when INSIDE a word. The written expression of these sounds differs to the written form of vowels when they come at the beginning or end of words instead following the above system of formulas. You can practice yourself on the worksheets in this book taking a consonant like फ् ph and going through the formulas to attach all the vowels अ a to अः aḥ and practice writing and saying the sounds.

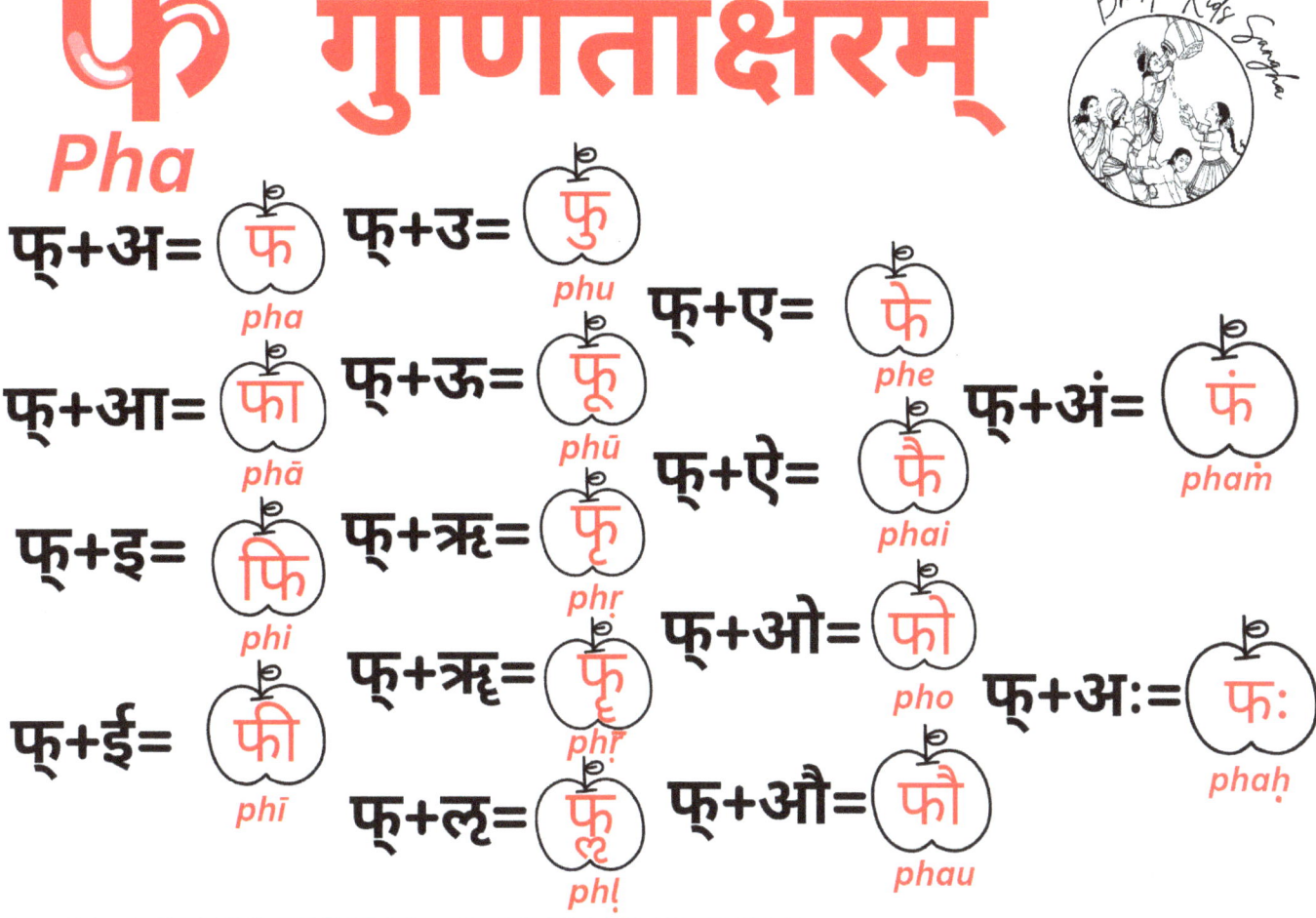

Half syllables
अर्धाक्षरम्
ardhākṣaram

क Ka	क् k	क् k
Full syllable	Base Syllable	Half Syllable
pūrṇākṣaram	mūlākṣaram	ardhākṣaram
consonant	For forming	forming compound
contains a	dependant vowels	consonants
a vowel.	guṇitākṣaram	samyuktākṣaram

We know that a consonant must contain a vowel to be a full consonant. We have also learned that a halanta removes a vowel from a consonant creating a base to be paired with other vowels (dependent vowels). To make compound consonants we must first understand half syllables or ardhākṣaram. Half syllables are forms of consonants that are incomplete, they do not contain a vowel and can be added to other consonants to make new shapes and sounds or phonemes.

अर्धाक्षरम्
ardhākṣaram
Half syllables

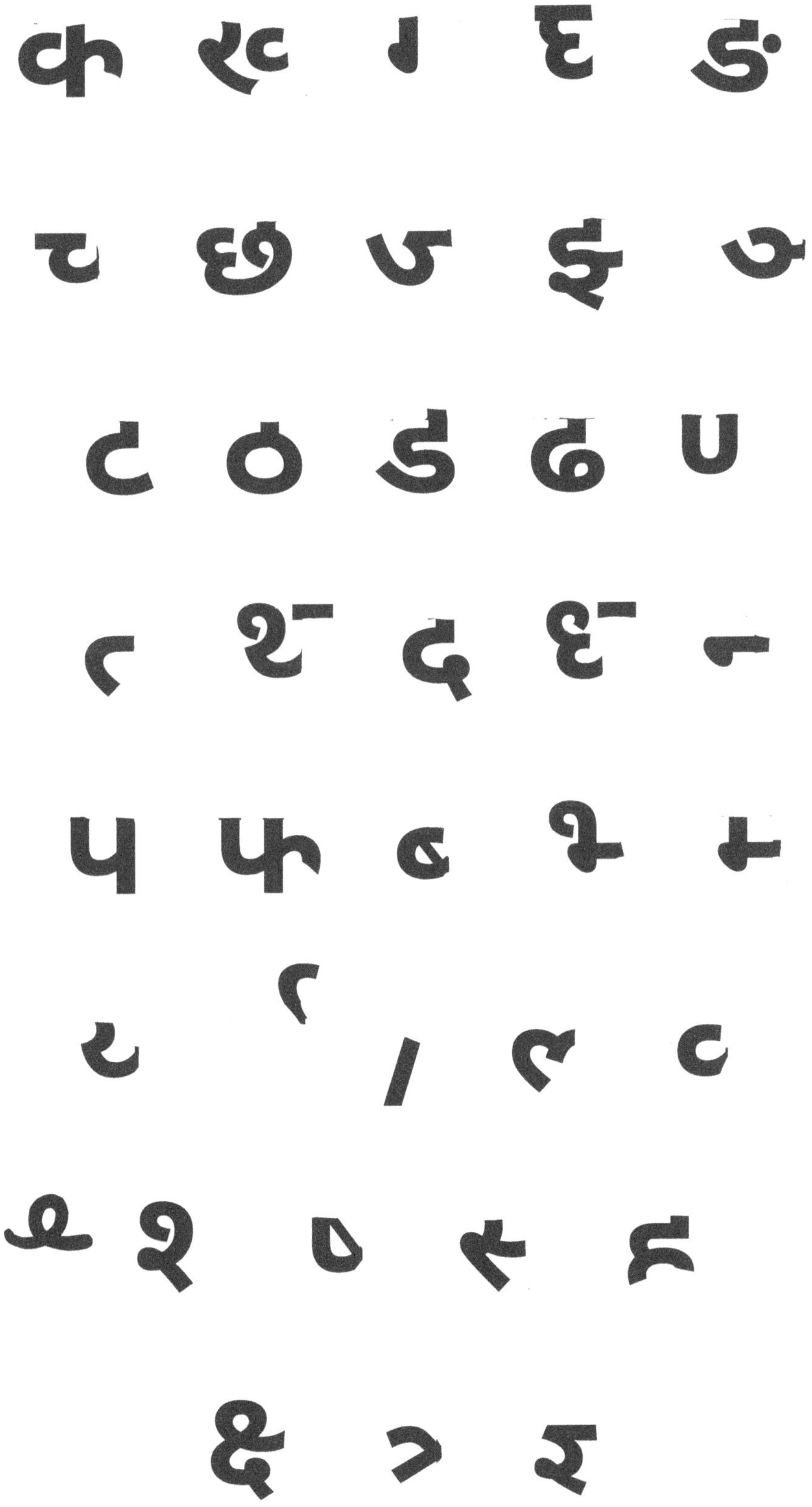

क् = क्‍	ख् = ख्‍	ग् = ग्‍	घ् = घ्‍	ङ् = ङ्‍
च् = च्‍	छ् = छ्‍	ज् = ज्‍	झ् = झ्‍	ञ् = ञ्‍
ट् = ट्‍	ट् = ट्‍	ड् = ड्‍	ढ् = ढ्‍	ण् = ण्‍
त् = त्‍	थ् = थ्‍	द् = द्‍	ध् = ध्‍	न् = न्‍
प् = प्‍	फ् = फ्‍	ब् = ब्‍	भ् = भ्‍	म् = म्‍
य् = य्‍	र् = र्‍ /	ल् = ल्‍	व् = व्‍	
श् = श्‍	ष् = ष्‍	स् = स्‍	ह् = ह्‍	
क्ष् = क्ष्‍	त्र् = त्र्‍	ज्ञ् = ज्ञ्‍		

In summary:
Every consonant has a broken form (see table) losing its vowel. We use these broken forms to attach together with another consonant to create a new sound or phoneme altogether. In this way we use ardhākṣaram (half syllables) to create samyuktākṣaram (compound consonants). Memorise these ardhākṣaram forms of the consonants to help you read and write words containing compound consonants.

Compound Consonants
संयुक्ताक्षरम्
Samyuktākṣaram

We have looked at vowels (svaraḥ), consonants (vyanjañam) in detail in the first two books. In this book we have looked at how consonants क् k - ह् h can be paired with all the vowels अ a - अः aḥ to form new sounds called dependant vowels (guṇitākṣaram). We also looked at half syllables (ardhākṣaram) which are essential for forming compound consonants.

We use the ardhākṣaram forms that do not contain a vowel, and add them to another consonant to form compound consonants.

In this example क् k has come without a vowel and attached to य् y who contains a short अ a to make a new sound क्य kya.

म् m has come without a vowel and attached to भ् bh who contains a short अ a to make a new sound म्भ mbha

त् t as come without a vowel and attached to प् p who contains a long आ ā to make a new sound त्पा tpā

च् c has come without a vowel and attached to छ् ch who contains a short अ a to make a new sound च्छ ccha

ङ् ṅ has come without a vowel and attached to ग् g who contains a short अ a to make a new sound ङ्ग ṅga

म् m as come without a vowel and attached to र् r who contains a short अ a to make a new sound म्र mra

ञ् ñ has come without a vowel and attached to ज् j who contains a short अ a to make a new sound ञ्ज ñja

ध् + न् + अ = ☐

प् + प् + अ = ☐

त् + प् + अ = ☐

स् + त् + अ = ☐

ब् + द् + अ = ☐

ष् + ण् + अ = ☐

च् + च् + अ = ☐

ज् + व् + अ = ☐

प् + म् + अ = ☐

ख् + य् + अ = ☐

Try forming compound consonants by studying the split strategy and applying what you have learned from all three books in this series.

Try forming compound consonants by studying the split strategy and applying your knowledge half syllables and dependant vowels.

श् ś has come without a vowel and attached to च् c who contains a short अ a to make a new sound श्च śca.

म् m as come without a vowel and attached to र् r who contains a short अ a to make a new sound म्र mra.

य् y has come without a vowel and attached to र r who contains a short अ a to make a new sound य्र yra.

न् n has come without a vowel and attached to न् n who contains a short अ a to make a new sound न्न nna.

ष् ṣ as come without a vowel and attached to ठ ṭh who contains a short अ a to make a new sound ष्ठ ṣṭha.

ट् ṭ has come without a vowel and attached to य् y who contains a short अ a to make a new sound ट्य ṭya.

ङ् ṅ has come without a vowel and attached to ग् g who contains a short अ a to make a new sound ङ्ग ṅga

ङ् ṅ as come without a vowel and attached to क् k who contains a short अ a to make a new sound ङ्क ṅka

श् ś has come without a vowel and attached to व् v who contains a short अ a to make a new sound श्व śva.

म् m has come without a vowel and attached to भ् bh who contains a short अ a to make a new sound म्भ mbha

त् t as come without a vowel and attached to प् p who contains a long आ ā to make a new sound त्पा tpā. In this example we see compound consonants and dependant vowels.

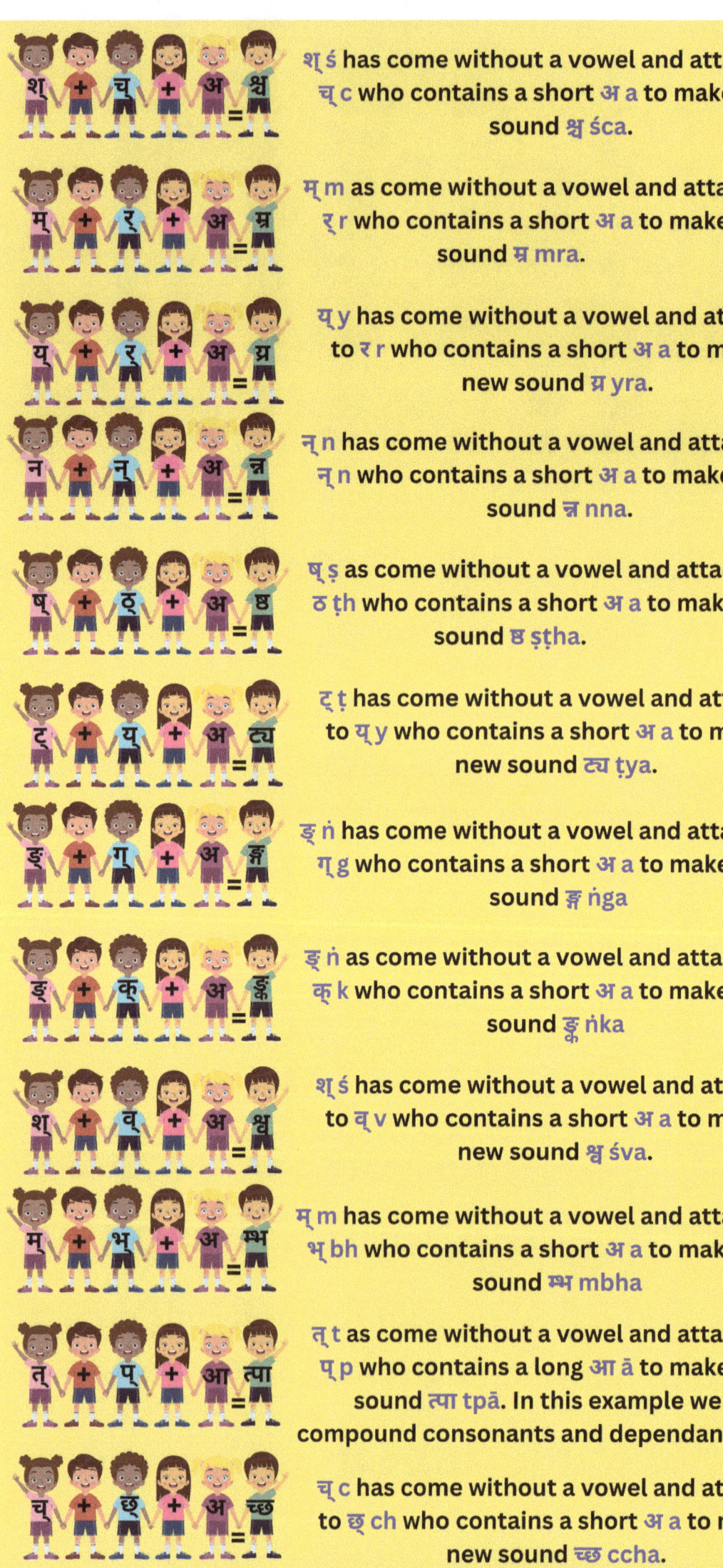

च् c has come without a vowel and attached to छ् ch who contains a short अ a to make a new sound च्छ ccha.

क + क् + उ = क्कु

क् k
Half Syllable
ardhākṣaram
Does Not
contain a
vowel

क् k
Base Syllable
mūlākṣaram
For forming
guṇitāksaram

उ u
Short vowel
hṛsva-Svaraḥ
to complete
the
consonant

कुक्कुटः
kukkuṭaḥ

क + क् + आ = क्का

क् k
Half Syllable
ardhākṣaram
Does Not
contain a
vowel

क् k
Base Syllable
mūlākṣaram
For forming
guṇitāksaram

आ ā
Long vowel
dīrga-Svaraḥ
to complete
the
consonant

ढक्का
ḍhakkā

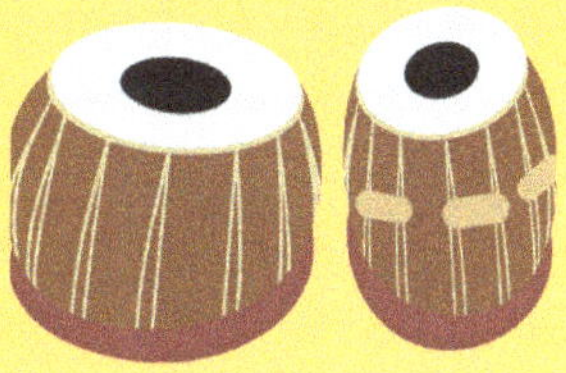

Above are two detailed examples of words containing a half syllable (ardhākṣaram) being added to consonant to create compound consonant (samyuktākṣaram) complete with a dependent vowel (guṇitākṣaram).

Now that we understand how compound consonants are formed let us learn the final group (three syllables) of the varṇamālā.

These compound consonants are so common they have their own shapes.

Compound -kṣa

क्ष

Compound consonant

क् k + ष् ṣ + अ a = क्ष kṣa

क्षत्रिय
kṣatriya
Warrior

क्षेत्रम्
kṣetram
Field

क्षीरम्
kṣīram
Milk

The compound consonant group is the final group of the varṇamālā.

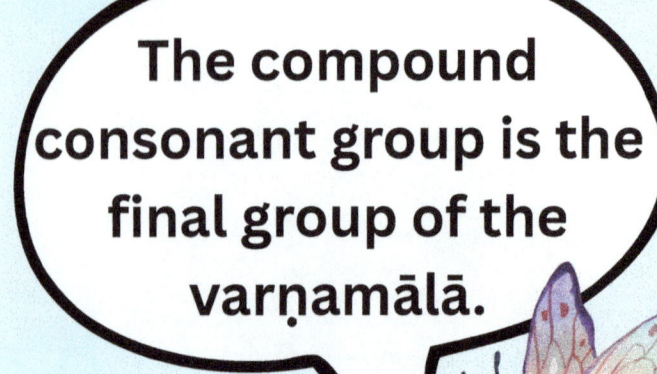

Compound -tra

त्र

Compound Consonant

त् t + र् r + अ a = त्र tra

सूत्रम्
sūtram
Thread

चित्रम्
citram
Picture

पुत्रः
putraḥ
Son

compound consonants can be formed using the information in this book.

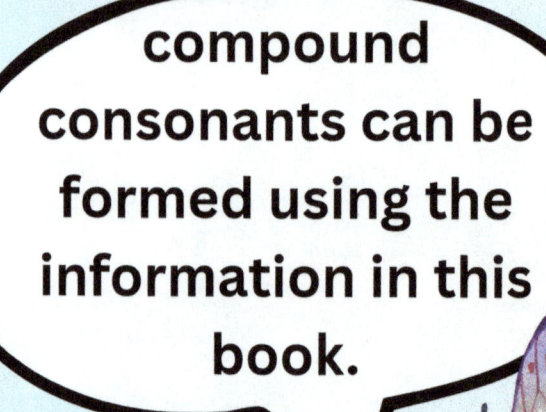

Compound jña

ज्ञ

Compound Consonant

ज् j + ञ् ñ + अ a = ज्ञ jña

ज्ञानम्
jñānam
Knowledge

प्रज्ञा
prajñā
Wisdom
Insight

राज्ञी
rājñī
Queen

Sorting phonemes

Identify the sounds and colour code using the key

= Vowel svaraḥ	= Consonant vyañjanam
= Base Syllable mūlākṣaram	= Dependant Vowel Gunitākṣaram
= Compound Consonant Samyuktākṣaram	

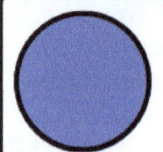

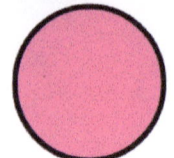

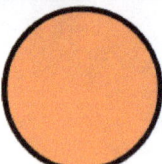

Sanskrita Varṇamālā Terminology glossary

Garland of syllables: वर्णमाला varṇamāla

Vowel: स्वरः svaraḥ

Vowels: स्वराः svarāḥ

Consonant: व्यञ्जनम् vyañjanam

Consonants: व्यञ्जनानि vyañjanāni

Letter: अक्षरम् akṣaram

Letters: अक्षराणि akṣarāṇi

Full syllable: पूर्णाक्षरम् pūrṇākṣaram

Base Syllable: मूलाक्षरम् mūlākṣaram

Half syllable: अर्धाक्षरम् ardhākṣaram

Dependant vowel:

गुणिताक्षरम् guṇitākṣaram

Compound consonant:

संयुक्ताक्षरम् saṃyuktākṣaram

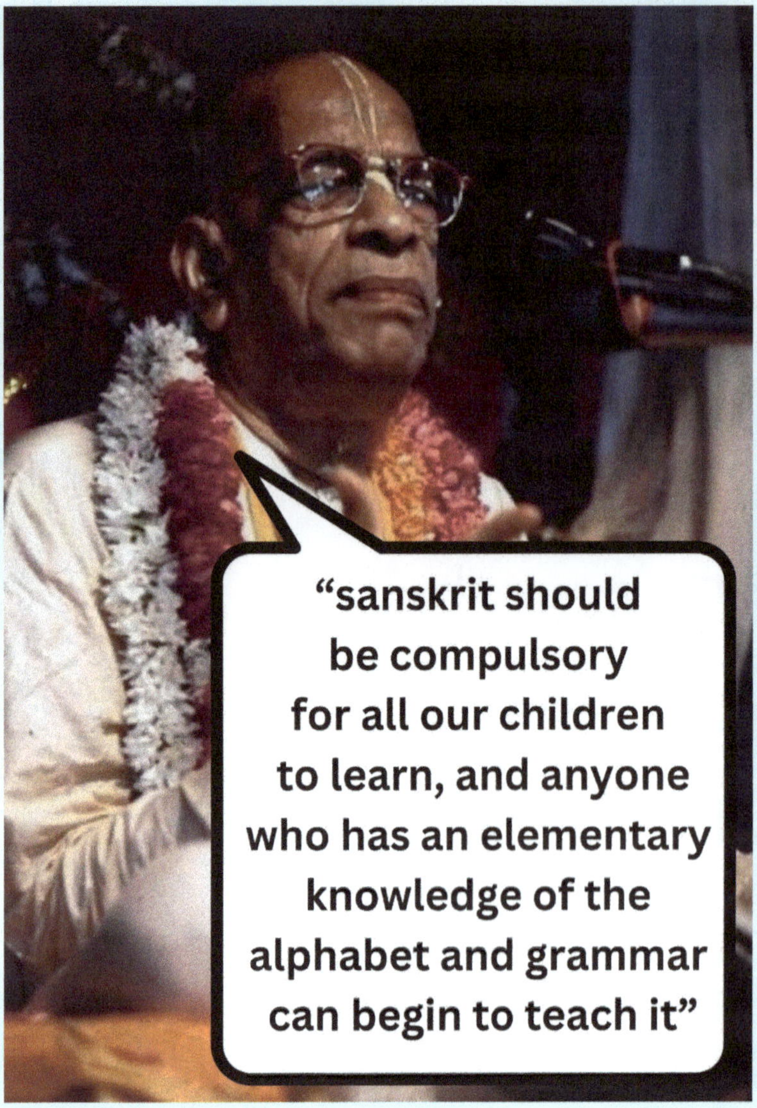

"sanskrit should be compulsory for all our children to learn, and anyone who has an elementary knowledge of the alphabet and grammar can begin to teach it"

The author

Abhidheya Devī Dāsī (Alice Goulding) is a mother of two and founder of Bhakti Kids Saṅgha. She teaches workshops , runs a podcast and teaches Sanskrit. She believes mother is the first guru of the child and that parents can take an active role in their child's spiritual life. It was Śrīla Prabhupāda's wish for all children to learn Sanskrit so she creates resources and teaches to fulfil this instruction.

9 781326 445461

www.ingramcontent.com/pod-product-compliance
Lightning Source LLC
Chambersburg PA
CBHW040403010726
47475CB00041BA/521
* 9 7 8 1 3 2 6 4 4 5 4 6 1 *